P9-AQQ-844

DUE

OFFICIALLY WITHDRAWN
N HAVEN FREE PUBLIC LIBRARY

FAIR HAVEN BRANCH
182 GRAND AVENUE
NEW HAVEN, CT 06513

Revised Edition

Derek Jeter

By Sandy Donovan

AMAZING ATHLETES

Lerner Publications Company • Minneapolis

Copyright © 2011 by Sandy Donovan

All rights reserved. International copyright secured. No part of this book may be reproduced, stored in a retrieval system, or transmitted in any form or by any means—electronic, mechanical, photocopying, recording, or otherwise—without the prior written permission of Lerner Publishing Group, Inc., except for the inclusion of brief quotations in an acknowledged review.

Lerner Publications Company
A division of Lerner Publishing Group, Inc.
241 First Avenue North
Minneapolis, MN 55401 U.S.A.

Website address: www.lernerbooks.com

Library of Congress Cataloging-in-Publication Data

Donovan, Sandra, 1967-
  Derek Jeter / by Sandy Donovan. — Rev. ed.
      p. cm. — (Amazing athletes)
  Includes bibliographical references and index.
  ISBN 978-0-7613-7065-9 (library binding : alk. paper)
  1. Jeter, Derek, 1974—Juvenile literature. 2. Baseball players—United States—Biography—Juvenile literature. I. Title.
  GV865.J48D66 2011
  796.357092—dc22 [B]   2010016833

Manufactured in the United States of America
1 – BP – 12/15/10

TABLE OF CONTENTS

Five-Time Champ   4

Young Yankees Fan   8

Becoming a Yankee   12

Rookie of the Year   16

Off the Field   20

Yankee Legend   24

Selected Career Highlights   29

Glossary   30

Further Reading & Websites   31

Index   32

Derek throws the ball to first base during Game 6 of the 2009 **World Series**.

FIVE-TIME CHAMP

Derek Jeter stood with his foot on second base. He stared straight at the pitcher. The New York Yankees **shortstop** and team captain knew he couldn't relax for even a second. Derek's teammate Hideki Matsui was at bat. Matsui was one of the team's best hitters. He had already hit a **home run** earlier in the game.

Derek has a career batting average of .321 in World Series games. This is the fourth highest average among players with at least 100 at bats.

Derek and the Yankees were playing Game 6 of the 2009 **World Series** against the Philadelphia Phillies. The Yankees led the series three games to two. If they could win Game 6, New York would be world champions.

Crack! Matsui swung and the ball exploded from his bat. Derek was running hard as the ball sailed into the outfield. He sprinted across home plate before the Phillies could stop him. The Yankees had the lead, 4–1.

Derek and the Yankees scored two runs in the fifth inning.

Derek came to bat again in the fifth inning. He swung hard and hit a **double**. Derek was back on second base. He came home to score when first baseman Mark Teixeira smacked the ball into the outfield. The Yankees were ahead, 5–1. The Phillies fought back, but they couldn't catch the Yankees. New York won the game and became World Series champions! With this victory, the Yankees have won the World Series 27 times. This is more than any other team. Derek has won the title with the Yankees five times. But each world championship is special. "This is what you dream of as a kid," Derek said after Game 6. "It doesn't get any bigger than this. You've got to enjoy it when the spotlight is on."

Derek holds the World Series trophy.

Derek and his family moved to Kalamazoo, Michigan, when he was four years old.

YOUNG YANKEES FAN

Derek Jeter was always a New York Yankees fan. He was born on June 26, 1974, in Pequannock, New Jersey, not far from New York City. His whole family—parents, grandparents, aunts, uncles, and cousins—were Yankees fans.

When Derek was four years old, he moved to Kalamazoo, Michigan, with his mother, Dorothy, and father, Charles. But Derek's love for the Yankees stayed with him. He covered his new bedroom with Yankees posters. He wore his blue Yankees jacket every day.

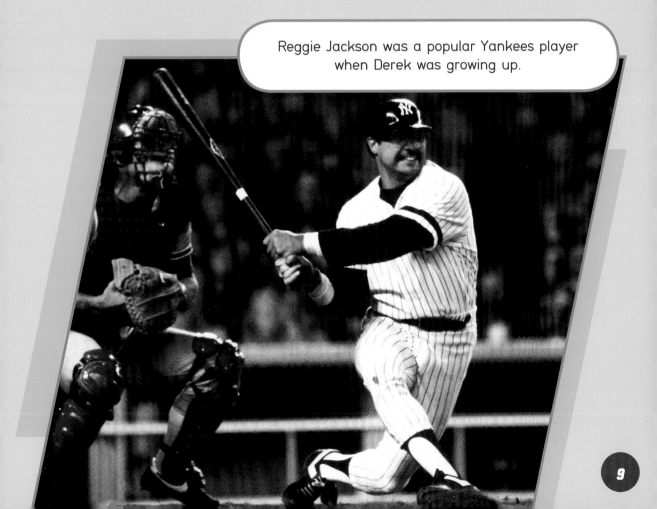

Reggie Jackson was a popular Yankees player when Derek was growing up.

Some of baseball's greatest players have worn the Yankees' uniform. They include Babe Ruth, Joe DiMaggio, Lou Gehrig, Mickey Mantle, Reggie Jackson, and Roger Clemens. Yankee great Dave Winfield was one of Derek's favorite players.

Every summer, Derek visited his grandparents in New Jersey. In 1980, when he was six, his grandmother took him to his first game at Yankee Stadium.

But Derek knew he wanted to be more than a Yankees fan. He wanted to be a Yankees player. In his eighth-grade yearbook, he wrote that he would play for the Yankees one day. Playing for the Yankees was Derek's **goal**.

Derek told his parents that he wanted to play shortstop for the Yankees. They told him he would have to work hard to reach this goal. But they said he could not just focus on baseball. He had to work hard at school too.

Derek did work hard. In high school, he got mostly A's. He practiced baseball every day. His family helped him. Dorothy, Charles, and Derek's younger sister, Sharlee, would play ball with him for hours.

Derek's biggest fans are his father, Charles; his sister, Sharlee; and his mother, Dorothy.

Derek was considered one of the best high school baseball players in the country.

BECOMING A YANKEE

In high school, Derek was a star baseball player. During his last two seasons, he hit better than .500. **Scouts** for **Major League Baseball** teams came to see him play in nearly every game. Some scouts thought Derek was the best high school player in the country.

Many high school coaches felt the same way. In his senior year, Derek was named the 1992 Player of the Year by the American Baseball Coaches Association. It looked as if he would be **drafted** by, or picked to join, a major-league organization.

Every year, Major League Baseball holds a draft. Each team takes turns drafting players. In 1992, the Cincinnati Reds had the first pick. Many people thought the Reds would choose Derek.

The Yankees drafted Derek soon after he graduated from high school.

But the Reds picked a different player. Instead, Derek got a surprise phone call. The New York Yankees called to say they had drafted him. Derek could not believe it. Was his dream of playing for the Yankees about to come true?

> Minor-league teams have different classes. Young, inexperienced players usually begin on a Class A team. As they get better, they move to Class AA. Class AAA teams are the closest step to the major leagues.

Hundreds of players are drafted each year. But only a few make it to the major leagues. Derek would have to work hard in the **minor leagues** to earn a spot with the Yankees.

Derek went to play for the Yankees' Class A team, the Tampa Yankees. He was full of excitement. But he was soon homesick for his family. He had never been so far away from them.

Derek had a rocky start in the minor leagues. During his first two years, he struggled with his batting and fielding. But Derek worked hard and became a better player. In 1994, the Yankees moved him up to their Class AA team. His batting average soared to .377. He was becoming a whiz at shortstop too. Derek was beginning to look like a star.

The Yankees played in this stadium from 1923 to 2008. A new Yankee Stadium opened in 2009.

ROOKIE OF THE YEAR

By 1995, Derek was playing for the Yankees' Class AAA team. That season, he also got his first taste of the big leagues. Derek played fifteen games for the Yankees. After the season, he was determined to make it back to the big leagues. That winter break, he practiced every day. During **spring training**,

Derek impressed Yankees manager Joe Torre so much that Torre gave Derek the starting shortstop job.

Derek quickly proved that Torre had made the right choice. During the first game of the 1996 season, Derek smashed a home run over the left field fence. He also made a difficult over-the-shoulder catch. His plays helped the Yankees beat the Cleveland Indians.

Joe Torre is admired for his instincts as a team manager. His hunch about Derek quickly paid off.

Derek continued to impress fans and players in his rookie year. In July, he got a hit in 17 straight games. His skill at the plate and on the field helped carry the Yankees to the **playoffs**. They played in the American League Championship Series against the Baltimore Orioles. Derek had a .412 batting average. The Yankees beat the Orioles. In his first year in the majors, Derek helped lead his team to the World Series.

In 1996, Derek became the first rookie in 34 years to be the Yankees' starting shortstop.

The Yankees went to the 1996 World Series against the Atlanta Braves, the defending champions. In the first two games at Yankee Stadium, the Braves outscored the Yankees 16–1.

The series seemed lost as the Yankees headed to Atlanta for the next three games. But the Yankees bounced back and won all three games in Atlanta. Back in New York, the Yankees won Game 6. It was their first World Championship since 1978. Derek was voted Rookie of the Year.

Derek *(right)* cheers as the Yankees tag out another Brave during the 1996 World Series.

Derek signs autographs for fans at Fenway Park in Boston.

OFF THE FIELD

Derek became one of the most popular Yankees. Letters from baseball fans piled up in his locker. But Derek wanted to make a difference off the field as well as on it.

After the 1996 season, Derek began a new project. He started the Turn 2 Foundation. (To "turn 2" means to make a **double play** in baseball.) Derek's group raises money to help keep kids away from drugs. It encourages kids to be healthy and to do well in school. The foundation pays for after-school programs, park festivals, and scholarships.

Derek wanted to show kids with problems at home or in school that they could work for success. Derek's father, Charles, is Turn 2's director. Derek said he has always looked up to his father. Charles worked for years helping other people as a drug and alcohol counselor.

Charles and Derek work together on the Turn 2 Foundation's programs.

Derek throws to first base for a double play in 1997.

Derek's work in the community is an important part of his life. "People look up to you if you play for the Yankees," he said. "I think you should do something to help out. Off the field is when people look up to you even more."

In 1997, Derek and the rest of the Yankees had a good year. They made the playoffs but lost to the Cleveland Indians in the first round. Still, Derek was proud of his team, and he was proud of his community work. He kept practicing to improve his play on the field. When they arrived for spring training in 1998, Derek and the Yankees were ready for a big year.

Derek fields a ground ball during spring training. The Yankees train in Tampa, Florida, at George M. Steinbrenner Field.

Derek *(left)* and Cleveland Indians shortstop Omar Vizquel *(right)* goof off before the 1999 All-Star Game.

YANKEE LEGEND

Derek and the Yankees steamrolled through the league from 1998 through 2000. They won the World Series all three years. They became the first major-league team in almost 30 years to "three-peat."

In 2001, the Yankees again made it to the World Series. But they lost to the Arizona Diamondbacks in a seven-game series.

Derek and the Yankees were disappointed in 2002 when they lost the American League Division Series to the Anaheim (later Los Angeles) Angels. Derek helped the Yankees reach the World Series again in 2003. But the Florida Marlins won the World Championship in six games.

Derek and the Yankees lost Game 7 of the 2001 World Series 3–2.

The Yankees were back in the American League Championship Series in 2004. They crushed the Boston Red Sox in the first three games. New York was one win away from returning to the World Series. But then something amazing happened. The Red Sox won the next four games to take the series!

The Yankees were knocked out of the playoffs each of the next three years. In 2008, New York didn't make the playoffs at all. The Yankees were frustrated.

To help the team return to the top, New York added three superstars before the start of the 2009 season. Pitchers A. J. Burnett and

In 2006 and 2009, Derek was the starting shortstop for Team USA in the World Baseball Classic. Team USA fought hard but came up short. Japan won both tournaments.

CC Sabathia, along with first baseman Mark Teixeira, all signed huge **contracts** with the Yankees.

On September 11, 2009, Derek passed the legendary Lou Gehrig as the all-time leader in hits for the Yankees. Gehrig had held the record for more than 70 years. Derek was humble about the honor. "I never imagined, I never dreamt of this," he said later.

Derek tips his helmet to the crowd after breaking Lou Gehrig's record.

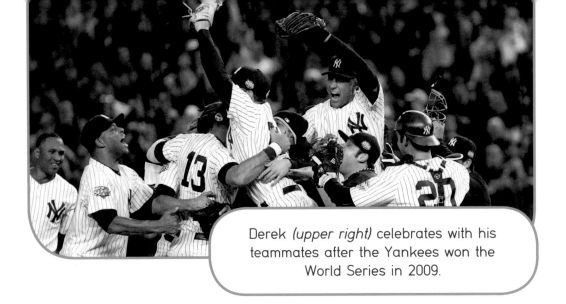

Derek *(upper right)* celebrates with his teammates after the Yankees won the World Series in 2009.

New York surged to the best record in baseball in 2009. With the help of their new players, the Yankees took care of business against the Phillies in the World Series.

Despite all his success, Derek doesn't take the World Series for granted. "You realize how difficult it is to get here," he said after winning the title in 2009. "I never lost sight of the fact that it's very difficult to get to the World Series, let alone win one." With Derek as captain, the Yankees are a good bet to win the championship again.

Selected Career Highlights

2009 Named *Sports Illustrated* Sportsman of the Year
Passed Lou Gehrig on Yankees' all-time hit list

2008 Named to All-Star team for ninth time

2007 Had a .322 batting average, ninth highest in the American
League

2006 Had a .343 batting average, second highest in the American
League

2005 Won his second Gold Glove Award

2004 Won his first Gold Glove Award

2003 Named team captain

2002 Played on his fifth consecutive All-Star team
Collected his 1,200th career hit and 100th home run

2001 Scored his 500th run on April 23, becoming the fourth Yankee
ever to reach 500 runs before his 26th birthday
Became the third Yankee ever to have more than 200 hits
three years in a row

2000 Helped Yankees beat their hometown rivals, the
New York Mets, to win the World Series for the
third year in a row
Named World Series MVP

1999 Had a .349 batting average, second highest in
the American League
Part of Yankee team that swept the Atlanta
Braves to win their 25th World Series

1998 Led the American League in runs scored with 127
Part of Yankee team that swept the San Diego
Padres in the World Series

1997 Tied the American League high of 142
singles in a season

1996 Hit a home run on opening day
Won American League Rookie of the
Year award

Glossary

at bats: a batters' official turn at the plate during games. If the batter walks, sacrifices, or is hit by a pitch, the turn is not counted as an at bat.

batting average: a number that describes how often a baseball player makes a base hit

contract: a written agreement between a player and a team. The contract says how much the player will be paid over a certain number of years.

double: play in which the batter hits the ball and safely reaches second base

double play: a play in which two base runners are thrown or tagged out

drafted: to be picked by a ball club to play on a team

goal: something a person works hard to achieve

home run: a hit that allows the batter to circle all the bases in one play to score a run

Major League Baseball: the top group of professional baseball teams. Major League Baseball has two leagues, the American League and the National League. The New York Yankees play in the American League.

minor leagues: leagues ranked below the major league. Players improve their playing skills in the minors and prepare to move to the majors.

playoffs: a series of games played after a regular season to determine which teams will play in a championship

scouts: people who search around the country for talented baseball players. Scouts recommend players they think teams should try to draft or sign.

shortstop: a player who plays in the field between second and third base

spring training: a period from February to April when teams practice for the upcoming season

World Series: baseball's championship. In Major League Baseball, the National League and the American League both hold their own league championships at the end of the regular season. The winning teams from each league meet each other in the World Series.

Further Reading & Websites

Christopher, Matt. *On the Field with Derek Jeter*. New York: Little, Brown, and Co., 2000.

Kennedy, Mike, and Mark Stewart. *Long Ball: The Legend and Lore of the Home Run*. Minneapolis: Millbrook Press, 2006.

Roth, B. A. *Derek Jeter: A Yankee Hero*. New York: Grosset & Dunlap, 2009.

Zuehlke, Jeffrey. *Alex Rodriguez*. Minneapolis: Lerner Publications Company, 2009.

Major League Baseball
http://www.mlb.com
Major League Baseball's official website has baseball news, games, and events. The Kids section has interviews with star players and "Tips from the Pros." You can also learn where to send letters to your favorite players.

New York Yankees' Home Page
http://newyork.yankees.mlb.com
The official website of the New York Yankees features the latest news, as well as the history of the team. The Players section includes Derek Jeter's biography, statistics, and career highlights.

Sports Illustrated Kids
http://www.sikids.com
The *Sports Illustrated Kids* website covers all sports, including baseball.

Turn 2 Foundation
http://www.turn2foundation.org
The official home page of Derek Jeter's foundation includes a list of events and programs. A special kids' section features games, a photo flip book, and a screen saver.

Index

American League Championship 18, 26

Burnett, A. J., 26

Derek Jeter: awards, 13, 19, 26; childhood, 8–10; drafted by Yankees, 14; in high school, 11–13; in minor leagues, 14–16; popularity of, 20; as team captain, 4, 28

Gehrig, Lou, 10, 27

Jeter, Charles (father), 9, 11
Jeter, Dorothy (mother), 9, 11
Jeter, Sharlee (sister), 11

Matsui, Hideki, 5

New York Yankees, 8–10, 13–17, 20, 22–24, 27–28; postseason, 4-7, 18–19, 22, 24–28

Ruth, Babe, 10

Sabathia, CC, 27

Tampa Yankees, 14
Teixeira, Mark, 6, 27
Torre, Joe, 17
Turn 2 Foundation, 20–21

Winfield, Dave, 10
World Championship, 7, 19, 25
World Series, 4–7, 18–19, 24–26, 28

Yankee Stadium, 10, 16, 18

Photo Acknowledgments

Photographs are used with the permission of: AP Photo/Julie Jacobson, p. 4; AP Photo/David J Phillip, p. 6; © Rob Trangali/SportsChrome, pp. 7, 19; © Stockphoto.com/Jane Tyson, p. 8; © Al Messerschmidt/Getty Images, p. 9; Jim Merihew/Kalamazoo Gazette, p. 11; Seth Poppel Yearbook Library, pp. 12, 13; © Joseph Sohm/Visons of America/CORBIS, p. 16; © MIKE FIALA/AFP/Getty Images, p. 17; © Reuters/CORBIS, pp. 20, 23; © John-Marshall Mantel, p. 21; AP Photo/Bill Kostroun, p. 22; © TIMOTHY CLARY/AFP/Getty Images, p. 24; AP Photo/Rusty Kennedy, p. 25; © Anthony J. Causi/Icon SMI, p. 27; UPI/John Angelillo/Newscom, p. 28.

Cover: AP Photo/Paul Sancya